IMAGINE LIVING HERE

# THIS PLACE IS HIGH

ILLUSTRATED BY
## BARBARA LAVALLEE

Walker and Company
New York

The author and artist gratefully acknowledge the support and assistance of the following: Eduardo Vera of the Peru Tourist Office, Alvaro Reyes of Lloyd Aero Boliviano, Reinaldo Pou Munt B. of Garza Tours, Dr. Benjamin Calvo P., Dr. Carlos Javier Ibarguen R., Dr. Vargas Eurique of IBBA, sociology professor Guanzalo Gautier G., Enrique Velardo Perez and Percy Salas Alford of Fondo de Promocion Turistoca in Cuzco, Enrique Salgado and the Hotel-Savoy Plaza, Naomi Fukuda of Foptur Lima, Juan Cornejo Pardo and Ramiro Cacon of Milla Tourism.

First published in the United States of America in 1989
by Walker Publishing Company, Inc.

Published simultaneously in Canada by Thomas Allen & Son
Canada, Limited, Markham, Ontario

The Library of Congress cataloged the cloth and reinforced editions of this book as follows:
Cobb, Vicki.
This place is high / by Vicki Cobb : illustrated by Barbara Lavallee.
p.   cm.—(Imagine living here)
Summary: Surveys the living conditions in the Andes Mountains of Bolivia for the people and unusual animals that live there.
ISBN 0-8027-6882-2.—ISBN 0-8027-6883-0 (lib. bdg.)
1. Andes Region—Description and travel—1981—Juvenile literature.   2. Man—Influence of environment—Andes Region—Juvenile literature.   3. Altitude, influence of—Andes Region—Juvenile literature.   [1. Andes Region—Description and travel.
2. Bolivia—Description and travel.]   I. Lavallee, Barbara, ill.
II. Title.   III. Series: Cobb, Vicki. Imagine living here.
F2212.C6   1989
980—dc20
89-32446
CIP
AC

ISBN 0-8027-7406-7 (paper)

Text design by Laurie McBarnette

Printed in Hong Kong

5   7   9   10   8   6   4

When you fly into La Paz, Bolivia, you land at El Alto, the highest airport in the world. El Alto are Spanish words meaning "the high one." The nearby snow-covered peaks of the Andes form a breathtaking skyline. But the view is not the only thing that takes your breath away.

This high up, almost two and a half miles above the sea, the air is "thin." There is less oxygen, and you will feel the first symptoms of mountain sickness—oxygen starvation— within five minutes after leaving your airplane. Your heart beats faster, you breathe more quickly, and a short staircase can leave you gasping. Within three hours you may have a pounding headache and feel sleepy. Some people get very sick and need to breathe pure oxygen to help them adjust to the thin air. Newcomers are advised to eat very little the first day, drink a special tea, and take it very easy for several days.

The Andes are high, rugged mountains running down the west coast of South America. They are the second highest mountains in the world after the Himalayas of Asia. About six hundred miles south of the equator, in central Peru, the Andes split and separate into two separate ridges. Between the ridges there is an enormous tableland called the *altiplano*, which means "high, flat land." The city of La Paz is located at the southern end of the altiplano in a circular valley. When you drive at night from the airport down to the city, it looks like a bowl of sparkling jewels.

More than a million people live in La Paz, the highest capital city in the world. The busy streets are full of traffic. The thin air puts a strain on the engines of ordinary cars. Gas doesn't provide cars with the same power it does at lower altitudes because it needs more oxygen. The cars here are adapted especially for thin air.

La Paz is near the equator, where the sun's rays are the strongest and most direct. The city is never very hot, though, because the higher you are above sea level, the cooler the air is. A sunny day here is usually a pleasant sixty-five degrees. But the temperature at night can be well below freezing. It is cold enough here to keep some of the higher mountains permanently covered with snow. Everyone wears warm clothing when the sun goes down. Uncomfortable winds whip across the altiplano at night that chap your hands and cheeks.

At sea level, the atmosphere normally blocks most of the sun's most dangerous rays. But here, since the highlands are closer to the sun, the rays pass through less air. More of the dangerous radiation reaches

the ground. You can quickly get a severe sunburn, especially if you are fooled by the cool air and don't cover up.

When you visit the highlands, your body slowly adjusts to the thin air. You make more red cells to carry more oxygen around the body. After a few days the symptoms of mountain sickness disappear. After six weeks, you will not notice any shortness of breath or a pounding heart during normal activities. But you will never be able run up and down the hills as easily or as long as the Indians born here.

On the other hand, when highlanders go down to sea level, they suffer from "lowlanders' sickness." Their hands and feet swell up. They are thirsty and sleepy and have no appetite.

A little more than half the people of the altiplano are native Aymara and Quechua (KESH-wah) Indians. Their skin is dark, which protects them from the sun's strong rays. Their barrel-shaped chests have larger lungs than people who live at sea level. Larger lungs can absorb more oxygen from the thin air. The Indians have about a quart more blood and many more red blood cells than lowlanders. Red blood cells carry oxygen, so Indian blood carries more oxygen than lowlanders. Their arms and legs are shorter, so blood can travel more quickly around the body. They have extra blood vessels in their hands and feet so they stay warm, even if they are barefoot, when it's freezing cold at night. Their hearts are larger and they pump more blood with each beat than smaller hearts. They don't notice that the air is thin.

The Bolivian altiplano is a harsh, treeless land. Since there is no wood, people build homes out of adobe, a sun-baked mixture of dirt and water. You can see stacks of adobe bricks here and there on the altiplano. Some of these are for sale, while others wait for their owners to build them into houses.

A hundred thousand years ago the altiplano was covered with ice. Ten thousand years ago the glaciers melted, forming a huge inland sea. Today, what is left of that sea is Lake Titicaca, the highest lake in the world large enough for steamships. It is more than one hundred miles long. When the Indians first drew a map of the lake, they decided that it had the shape of a puma, a kind of wildcat, jumping over a rabbit. So they named it Titicaca, which means "puma jumping over a rabbit."

Totora reeds grow in the shallow waters of the lake. They are extremely important to the Indians. The Indians pull up the reeds and pile them on the lake floor to build small islands to live on. They build houses out of the reeds and also feed them to their cattle. They save the tender roots of young totoras to eat themselves. And they weave the reeds together to make fishing boats. A reed boat takes two weeks to build and lasts about six months before it becomes too rotten to be safe. Many Indians who live on the lake earn a living fishing for the delicious, pink Lake Titicaca trout.

The most important animals on the altiplano are the llamas and alpacas, both distant relatives of the camel. Llamas are large enough to carry one-hundred-pound loads and have been used for transportation for thousands of years. They are very mean-tempered animals. If you load a llama with one pound more than it is willing to carry, it will spit with excellent aim. Llamas provide food, too. Their meat is salted and dried in the sun. The Indians call it charqui (CHAR-kee). That's where we get the word "jerky" for the dried beef we eat in North America.

Llama wool is coarse, good for blankets, not clothing. But the smaller alpacas are raised for their especially fine soft wool that sometimes grows long enough to reach the ground. The vicuña, a small wild relative, has the finest wool of all. It was hunted almost to extinction for its wool and is now protected by law.

Herds of llamas and alpacas graze on the altiplano. Different-colored tassels in the animals' ears identify their owners.

Two other animals of the Andes are the chinchilla and the guinea pig. Chinchillas are about 15 inches long and weigh just over two pounds. If you picked one up you might be surprised at how light it is. It looks as if it ought to weigh a lot more because its thick, silky fur is so fluffy. Wild chinchillas were hunted for their valuable fur until they were almost extinct. Now wild chinchillas are protected, and chinchilla farms supply the furriers.

Guinea pigs have been raised by Indians in the Andes for at least as long as they've raised llamas, more than two thousand years. Their meat is tender and delicious, similar to chicken.

The north end of the altiplano has valleys with steep mountainsides. You can't flatten a mountain, but you can farm it. How? By building flat steps, or terraces, up the mountainside. Long ago the Indians built stone walls and put in layers of rocks, stones, and sand for proper drainage, the way you prepare a large flower pot for planting. Then they added soil to make flat areas that could be planted. On the steepest slopes, the terraces might only be a few feet wide. Usually the walls are about fifteen feet high with large stepping stones sticking out so farmers can climb between terraces. Some of the terraces have small stone canals to direct springwater or rainwater to irrigate the crops.

Terraces built centuries ago are still being farmed today. Every once in a while, high on the hill, you'll see a small stone house, used to store part of the harvest. These stone houses are often within a day's walk of each other. This was done so that the ancient Incan armies would have food at the end of a day's march.

There are two crops that grow well at high altitudes. One is quinoa (KEEN-wah), a wheatlike grain that can be ground into flour. Grain is an important crop because the seeds can be stored from harvest to harvest without spoiling. A good supply of quinoa makes sure that people will not starve. Quinoa plants may be red, blue, or yellow. Fields of quinoa color the mountainsides.

The other crop is the potato. Three thousand years ago, small wild potatoes were developed into cultivated crops by the Indians. Today, more than two hundred different kinds of potatoes are grown in the Andes, including the white potato you know. Potatoes don't keep as well as grain, so the Indians have a special way of preserving them. Small potatoes are spread on the ground to freeze overnight. The next day the sun defrosts the frozen potatoes. The Indians stomp on them with bare feet, squeezing out the water and breaking off the skin. This process is repeated for several days. The result is naturally freeze-dried black potatoes called chuño (CHUN-yo), which will keep for several years.

Indians soak chuño in water for a week before cooking it in soups and stews over fires of dried llama dung. It takes a lot longer to cook potatoes in the highlands. The temperature of boiling water is about twenty-five degrees cooler than at sea level so potatoes have to be boiled longer to make them soft enough to eat.

What's for dinner? A typical meal is a delicious stew of llama meat, corn meal, barley, and chuño. A favorite dessert is a kind of popcorn that looks like giant snow-white kidney beans coated with sugar called pasankalla.

The Indians have a legend about the birth of their civilization. They believe that on the Island of the Sun in Lake Titicaca, the Sun God Inti created their first rulers, the Incas. Inti sent a man, named Manco Capac, and his wife to live on this island and teach people to build villages and grow crops. Then Inti gave the Inca couple a golden rod and told them to travel away from the island. "Wherever you stop to rest, try to throw this rod into the earth," he said to them. "Build your city at the place where it sinks into the soil with a single thrust." The place where the rod sank into the ground is several hundred miles north of the lake. Here the Indians built a city they called Cuzco, which means "the bellybutton of the world." They laid out the streets of Cuzco so that the city has the shape of a puma, the same shape as the larger section of Lake Titicaca.

The Indians believe that a long line of Inca rulers descended from Manco Capac and his wife. In 1438, the ninth Inca ruler, Pachacuti (Pah-chah-KOO-tee), came to power. His name means "he who changes the earth." Pachacuti and his son left Cuzco to conquer almost one hundred different Indian tribes to form the great Inca Empire called Tahuantinsuyu (Tah-wan-tin-SOO-yoo), which means "The Four Corners of the World." The Incas learned new skills in weaving, metal working, masonry, and ceramics from the tribes they conquered. These crafts added to the riches of the empire.

Over the next ninety-six years the Inca kings ruled an area twenty-five hundred miles long with up to twelve million people. Relay runners, stationed a mile and a half apart, carried messages across the empire. A message could travel about 250 miles a day.

Since wood was scarce, the Incas built their empire with stones. They built stone roads, temples, forts, and buildings. To protect Cuzco, Pachacuti continued the building of a great fortress started by the third Inca ruler. The stones they used as tools were even harder than the big building stones they were cutting. They would twist their stone drills with a mixture of sand and water to make holes in the building blocks. Then they used wedge-shaped stone hammers to break the blocks of stone along the line of holes, exactly as planned.

The Incas used stone ramps covered with mud to push the stones up hills. Then they built ramps of dirt to move them to the top of a wall being built. Once the stones were in place, they beat the walls with stone hammers to give it an even finish. When the building was finished the dirt ramps were removed.

Twenty thousand men worked every day for thirty years to build the fortress. The Inca Empire required young men to spend nine months a year working at government building projects. It was a tax that people paid in labor instead of money. In return the empire gave each man's family land to farm. One quarter of each family's crops went to the Incas for the gods, one quarter went for the poor and elderly who couldn't work, one quarter went for the army, and one quarter they could keep.

When you visit the Inca ruins more than five hundred years later, they are amazing to see. The perfectly cut stones of their important buildings fit together like a jigsaw puzzle. A dime couldn't slip between them. The Incas did not use mortar, like concrete, to hold the stones in place. The stones fit so closely they didn't need to.

The Incas built over ten thousand miles of roads, but they were only for the feet of people and llamas. They never invented the wheel, so they had no carts or wagons. They constructed rope bridges across steep canyons. Some of these foot bridges are still in use and must be replaced each year. The Incas also never developed a written language, but they kept track of people, crops, and animals with a system of knots tied in strings. The Incas also created beautiful objects of gold and silver to decorate their buildings. They didn't think gold and silver were valuable, they just liked the way the pretty metals looked. They said gold was the "sweat of the sun," and silver "the tears of the moon." But gold and silver eventually cost them their kingdom.

If you look at a plan of the city, the fortress would be the head of the puma. Some of the stones in its walls are huge, weighing more than three hundred tons. The Incas called them "weary stones" because they got weary dragging them with ropes from the quarries eighteen miles away.

There is a legend about a stone near the fortress that is bigger than a school bus. It was hauled from a quarry forty-five miles away. Three thousand men died moving it. By the time they reached the bottom of the hill of the fortress, they were too tired to move it any further. So they left it, and it's still there today.

In 1532, Francisco Pizarro, a Spanish ship captain, landed on the shores of Peru. He led his band of 168 men into the Inca Empire. The Spaniards conquered the Incas by capturing their ruler and frightening them with their horses and cannons, which the Incas had never seen. Without their ruler the people were disorganized and did what the Spaniards wanted. When rooms full of gold and silver were demanded as ransom for the Inca king, the Incas gave it to them. Buildings were looted anyway. By the middle of the next year, twenty-four tons of gold and silver were delivered to the Spaniards.

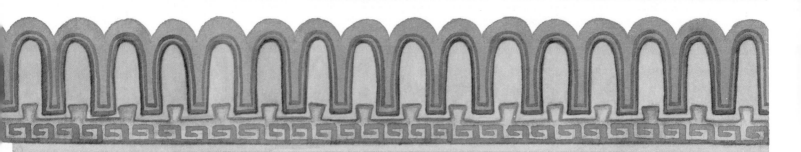

Over the next few years, some of the Incas resisted and fought back but they never regained their empire. The Spanish rule was complete. The Spaniards tore down the Inca buildings and used the stones to build their own churches. They left the Inca foundations, however, and built their own homes on top of them. Most of the buildings in Cuzco clearly show the boundary between the Inca stonework and the Spanish. Today, many people in Peru are a mixture of Indian and Spanish. There is a lot of pride in the Inca Empire and all that it accomplished in less than one hundred years. The ruins and the treasures that have survived are a constant reminder of the Incas' glorious past.

There is one Inca city that the Spanish never found and so did not destroy. It's called Machu Picchu (MA-choo PEE-choo), meaning "Old Peak," and it's easy to understand why no one found it. Machu Picchu is on top of a small but very steep mountain. The base of the mountain is low enough to be covered by jungle. Machu Picchu was built during Pachacuti's rule and abandoned around the time of the Spanish conquest. It is a mystery. No one knows why it was abandoned. It was connected to the city of Cuzco by seventy-six miles of stone roads. Over the years the roads were overgrown, the buildings lost their thatched roofs, and the jungle crept in to hide this mysterious city.

Hiram Bingham, an American explorer, found Machu Picchu in 1911. He called it the "Lost City of the Incas." Immediately scientists went to work digging it out. It is an incredible city of white granite. It has ten acres of terraced farmland that fed the city's population of one thousand people. Machu Picchu contains 263 buildings and more than three thousand steps, all made of hand-carved stone. Some of the buildings were homes, some stored food, and in the center stood a temple to the sun. All the buildings are in the Inca style. The walls tilt slightly in toward the roof, and doorways and windows are narrower at the top than at the bottom. The Incas discovered that this kind of structure would last through the many earthquakes that happen in the Andes. Most of the skeletons that were found there were female, so scientists think that the city may have been built for religious reasons, as a place for holy girls and women. Today, Machu Picchu is considered one of the world's great wonders.

The people who live on the altiplano are always busy doing something. There are no idle hands here. Children learn to spin yarn on single spindles they carry around with them. Women weave blankets to sell at the side of the roads. All the hand-knitted sweaters, hats, and scarves in the markets are produced by people knitting in their homes. The handicrafts show bold patterns and bright colors or the natural brown, black, and white of the alpaca. Their music is mostly the haunting tones of their flutes. The highlands of the Andes is a place for lovers of beauty, history, nature, and mystery. Can you imagine living here?